Read-About® Geography

Map Keys

By Rebecca Aberg

Consultant
Jeanne Clidas, Ph.D.
National Reading Consultant
and
Professor of Reading, SUNY Brockport

Children's Press®
A Division of Scholastic Inc.
New York   Toronto   London   Auckland   Sydney
Mexico City   New Delhi   Hong Kong
Danbury, Connecticut

Designer: Herman Adler Design
Photo Researcher: Caroline Anderson
The artwork on the cover shows a simple map and corresponding key.

Library of Congress Cataloging-in-Publication Data

Aberg, Rebecca.
  Map keys / by Rebecca Aberg.
      p. cm. — (Rookie read-about geography)
Includes index.
Summary: Introduces how to read and use a map key, and provides
instructions on how to create a map of one's own bedroom and a key to
its symbols.
  ISBN 0-516-22722-X (lib. bdg.)   0-516-27773-1 (pbk.)
  1. Map reading—Juvenile literature. 2. Maps—Symbols—Juvenile
literature. [1. Map reading. 2. Maps.] I. Title. II. Series.
  GA130 .A24 2003
  912'.01'4—dc21

                                        2002011535

CHILDREN'S PRESS, AND ROOKIE READ-ABOUT®,
and associated logos are trademarks and or registered trademarks
of Grolier Publishing Co., Inc. SCHOLASTIC and associated logos
are trademarks and or registered trademarks of Scholastic Inc.
6 7 8 9 10 R 12 11 10 09   46

What is a map key?

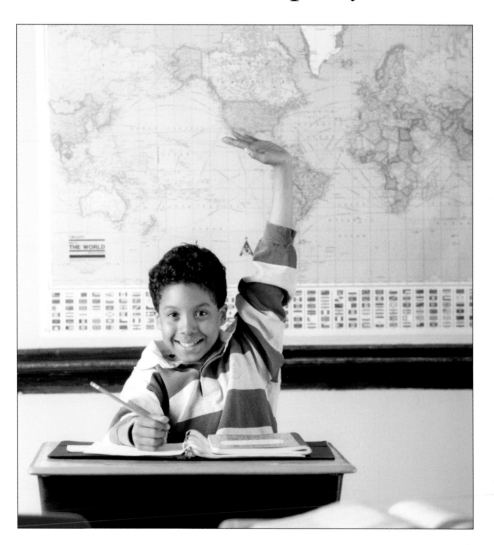

A map key is a box that is next to a map. It is also called a legend (LEG-uhnd).

5

MAP KEY

 airport

 fire station

 library

 school

 park

Pictures on maps are symbols (SIM-buhlz). A map key tells what the symbols mean.

Some symbols are pictures of things we know.

This map shows part of a town. Use the key to read the map.

What is the symbol for the school? Can you find the fire station?

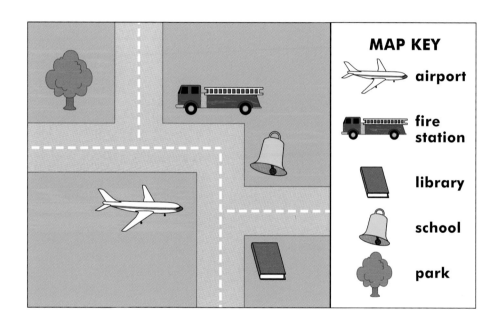

MAP KEY

airport

fire station

library

school

park

9

MAP KEY

○ campfire

▤ picnic table

▲ tent

10

Some symbols are shapes. The map key shows what each shape means.

This is a map of a campground. Triangles (TRIE-ang-guhls) stand for the tents. What do the circles stand for?

Other symbols are colors.
The map key shows what
each color means.

On this map, water is blue.
Cities are yellow. What
color is farmland?

MAP KEY

city

farmlands

forests

water

13

MAP KEY

▬ ▬ ▬ dirt road

•••••• hiking trail

main streets

╫╫╫╫ railroad tracks

Some maps use different kinds of lines as symbols. These lines stand for streets, hiking trails, and railroad tracks.

Look at this map and map key. What are the dotted lines? Can you find the railroad tracks?

Here is a map of a zoo.
Use the map key to find
Jungle Trail. What animals
will you see along the trail?

MAP KEY

bear

monkey

parrot

squirrel

forest path

jungle trail

17

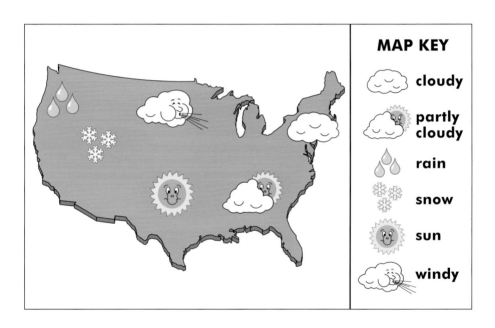

MAP KEY

cloudy

partly cloudy

rain

snow

sun

windy

18

Symbols on weather
(WHETH-ur) maps show
sun, clouds, rain, and snow.

Point to the places that
are sunny. Where is it
raining? What do the
snowflakes mean?

Maps of rooms are called floor plans. These maps look like you are looking down from the ceiling. The top of a table may look like a rectangle (REK-tang-guhl).

What shape are the student desks on this floor plan?

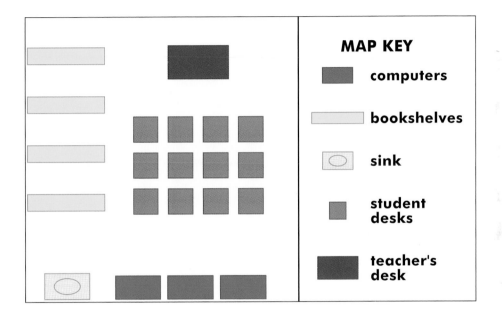

MAP KEY

- computers
- bookshelves
- sink
- student desks
- teacher's desk

21

MAP KEY

picnic table

pool

slide

swings

22

Some floor plans show
outdoor places.

Here is a map of a park.
What symbols stand for
the picnic tables? How
many slides do you see?

Maps are fun to make.
You can draw a map of
your bedroom.

What is the shape of your
room? What shapes and
colors will you use for
the things in your room?

MAP KEY

bed
bookcase
chair
desk
door
lamp
rug
table
window

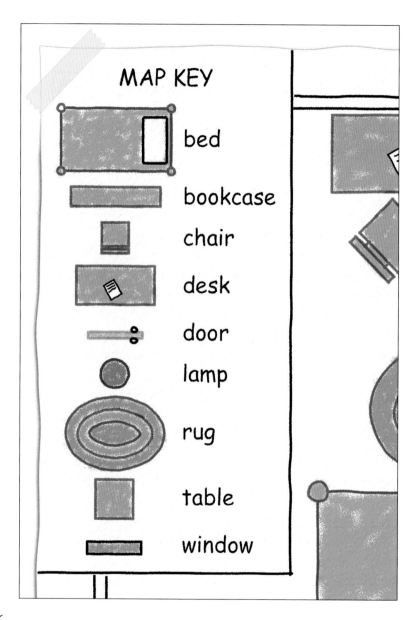

MAP KEY

bed

bookcase

chair

desk

door

lamp

rug

table

window

Don't forget to draw a map key for your bedroom map.

Use the same symbols you used on your map, only make them smaller. Write what each symbol means.

Now everyone can read your map.

Words You Know

floor plan

MAP KEY

- computers
- bookshelves
- sink
- student desks
- teacher's desk

map key

- airport
- fire station
- library
- school

symbols

30